Frederic Henry Gerrish

Prescription Writing

Designed for the Use of Medical Students who have never studied Latin

Frederic Henry Gerrish

Prescription Writing
Designed for the Use of Medical Students who have never studied Latin

ISBN/EAN: 9783742831842

Manufactured in Europe, USA, Canada, Australia, Japa

Cover: Foto ©Andreas Hilbeck / pixelio.de

Manufactured and distributed by brebook publishing software
(www.brebook.com)

Frederic Henry Gerrish

Prescription Writing

PRESCRIPTION WRITING.

DESIGNED FOR THE USE OF

MEDICAL STUDENTS WHO HAVE NEVER STUDIED LATIN.

BY

FREDERIC HENRY GERRISH, A.M., M.D.,

PROFESSOR OF ANATOMY AND FORMERLY PROFESSOR OF MATERIA MEDICA AND
THERAPEUTICS IN BOWDOIN COLLEGE, CONSULTING SURGEON TO THE
MAINE GENERAL HOSPITAL, SOMETIME PRESIDENT OF THE
MAINE STATE BOARD OF HEALTH, AND OF THE
AMERICAN ACADEMY OF MEDICINE, ETC.

Eighth and Revised Edition.

PORTLAND, ME.:

LORING, SHORT, AND HARMON.

PHILADELPHIA: J. B. LIPPINCOTT & CO.

1895.

CONTENTS.

PREFATORY NOTE

TO THE EIGHTH EDITION.

ALTHOUGH the only system of weights and measures employed in the Pharmacopœia of 1890 is the metric, it has seemed unwise to ignore the old method in these pages. This attitude cannot be ascribed to any fondness for the complicated and time-consuming system, or to any hostility to the simple and facile modern substitute, if one will observe the appendix, which was written fifteen years ago. Inasmuch, however, as but a small minority of our physicians and medical students are practically familiar with the metric system, its exclusive employment in this book would be almost certain to repel many of those for whose sake the little volume was written, and thus seriously impair its influence. The purpose in view is to teach a little Latin, not to promote the universal adoption of the decimal method, although that is a commendable application of effort.

PREFACE.

Every teacher of medicine in this country must have been impressed with the fact that a large proportion of the students in our schools have no knowledge of the Latin language. This is demonstrated daily by the difficulty with which they learn the technical names of the various structures, diseases, processes, and agents with which they have to deal, each being committed to memory arbitrarily, and affording no clue to any other term. In no other class of cases, however, is this deficiency of education so apparent as with regard to the terminology of the pharmacopœia, especially when it becomes necessary to make the grammatical changes required in giving directions for compounding medicines. Students are often deterred from undertaking the labor needed to make them expert in this respect, from a mistaken idea of its magnitude. It is to help them in this very important but much neglected part of their medical work that this little book has been written. It is not designed to give instruction in the art of prescribing, but simply to teach those who know nothing whatever of the language the little Latin which is essential to correct prescription writing, and to inculcate such lessons on this subject as a considerable experience in teaching has shown to be desirable. The first part contains the rules to be observed in writing prescriptions; the second part presents all the words that are necessary for (though not all that may be used in) this exercise, so arranged as best to facilitate reference and the easy acquirement of a sufficient familiarity with their various forms.

I am aware that it may be objected to this plan that it gives the student little more than a parrot-like command of a few words and expressions, and does not teach him the principles of the language. But I respectfully submit that it is far better for a man to write a prescription correctly, even in the most automatic way, than to blunder through it disgracefully, as so many habitually do, and thus expose himself to the ridicule of apothecaries' shop-boys. Besides, I cherish the not unreasonable hope that the aid in prescription writing derived from the little knowledge of Latin which this book may impart will so convince some students of the value of the language, that they will systematically undertake the mastery of its elements, and acquire a considerable vocabulary. The time is not very far off, I trust, when no one will be allowed to matriculate in a medical school who has not a good reading knowledge of easy Latin. Until then, it seems to me that such books as this is designed to be may perform an important service.

F. H. G.

PORTLAND, MAINE,
    31st of August, 1877.

PRESCRIPTION WRITING.

FIRST PART.

RULES FOR WRITING PRESCRIPTIONS.

THE word Prescription is derived from the Latin *præ*, meaning "before," and *scriptum* (the perfect participle of *scribo*, "I write"), meaning "written." It, therefore, etymologically signifies "something written beforehand," and thus preserves the memory of the custom which formerly obtained among physicians of writing down their advice for the guidance of their patients. Soon, however, the word came to be applied to any recommendation, whether written or spoken, which the medical attendant made. Thus, verbal directions about the food of the sick man, the ventilation or lighting of his room, the preservation of quiet, the change of linen, in short, all things which will in any way contribute to the restoration of his health, are prescriptions.

But, though this is a not infrequent use of the word, it has a restricted meaning which is much more common. It is employed to designate a formula consisting of directions to an apothecary concerning the compounding of a medicine, and in this sense only will it be used in this book.

It should be understood, to start with, that the object of this work is to give instruction in the art of writing prescriptions, and not in that of prescribing. The one may be learned in a very short time and with comparatively little labor; the other can be acquired only by prolonged study and experience with diseases and medicines. I take it for granted that the student has spent some time at his Materia Medica, and knows something of the principles of medicinal combination, of the incompatibilities of drugs, and of dosage. It may be well, however, to mention that the true type of a prescription is based upon a maxim of Asclepiades, *Curare cito, tuto et jucunde,* which proclaims the duty of the therapeutist to be to *Cure quickly, safely,* and *pleasantly.* This saying it is always well to bear in mind in prescribing, inasmuch as attention to its suggestions will guide the physician to the most advantageous administration of medicines. According to this rule, the typical prescription contains, first, an ingredient which is expected to do the chief work in the case, whose office it is to *cure* or relieve the patient, and which is hence called the BASIS; second, an element designed to assist or accelerate the action of the basis, to make it do its work more *quickly* than if left to itself, and therefore known as the ADJUVANT; third, a substance calculated to correct or modify some undesirable or injurious effect of the basis or the adjuvant, to cause it to act more *safely* than it would alone, and for this reason named the CORRIGENT; and, fourth and last, a material which will give such form and consistence to the preparation as to make it *pleasant,* or, at all events, not disagreeable, for the patient to take, a carrier of the active parts of the compound, and consequently designated the Excipient. This will be understood at once by a glance at the following table : —

Curare (Cure) with the Basis (the Essential).
Cito (Quickly) ,, ,, Adjuvant (the Assistant).
Tuto (Safely) ,, ,, Corrigent (the Corrective).
et
Jucunde (Pleasantly) ,, ,, Excipient (the Vehicle).

As an illustration, let us suppose that we desire to prescribe for a case of constipation in which the Compound Extract of Colocynth would be an appropriate remedy. Employing this as the Basis, we may assist its laxative action by associating with it a proper quantity of Blue Pill, which would be the Adjuvant. But Colocynth is liable to produce griping, and this tendency we can correct by employing the Extract of Henbane as a Corrigent. Finally, the addition of a little Syrup as Excipient will render it easy to make the whole into a pill-mass of proper consistency.

It must not be supposed that every correct prescription contains all these elements. Sometimes the Basis is all that is needed ; for it may alone be sufficiently powerful for the purpose required, may have no tendency to produce any unpleasant symptoms, and, at the same time, be naturally in a condition which renders it agreeable to take. In another case, the Basis may need an Adjuvant or a Corrigent or a Vehicle, or some two of these. The Basis is always present, it is essential ; the others may or may not be needed.

In prescribing, simplicity should be aimed at ; but one must guard against the extreme which, for the sake of simplicity, would violate the least important of the charges in the old precept which we have analyzed. " Never give a particle of medicine which is not required," is a rule which should have always as its companion, " Give whatever drugs are needed to cure quickly, safely, and pleasantly."

It is a good plan for a physician to keep about him a sufficient quantity of paper, cut into pieces of convenient size and shape, for writing prescriptions. One should never, when he can possibly avoid it, rely upon a chance supply, such as may be had at the houses of his patients. To say nothing of the inconvenience which such a practice may entail upon all concerned, it often obliges one to send out a slovenly-looking prescription, and it betrays a lack of that thoughtfulness about little things which is properly expected of a medical attendant. Pen and ink are preferable to pencil, as producing writing which is less liable to blurring and erasures, and therefore safer.

The writing should be so distinct that no word or symbol can possibly be mistaken for any other. Every letter even ought to be well defined. Sometimes it is a matter of literally vital moment that just what the physician intends by his prescription should be given to the patient; therefore it is a duty to cultivate the habit of legibility, that clearness may not be wanting when the greatest necessity for it arises. The chirography of some physicians is simply homicidal.

In prescribing unusually large doses of powerful medicines, which might alarm the druggist and cause him to hesitate about compounding the prescription, unless he were absolutely certain of the intent of the physician, it is well to write the quantities of the drugs in both Roman and Arabic characters. The apothecary will then have evidence that the dose was deliberately and carefully determined upon, and will without fear supply the patient immediately, and thus avoid a delay which, in an exigent case, might be disastrous.

Before it is parted with, a prescription should be carefully revised. Every item of it should be studiously scrutinized, to make sure of its correctness. He is a rare man who never makes a mistake ; and it is very curious to see how strangely astray physicians will sometimes go in their prescriptions, writing for articles which are furthest from their thoughts, ordering ounces for drachms, and *vice versa*, leaving out the directions for quantities altogether, omitting to state the size and time of the dose, and otherwise giving evidence of wandering attention and deficient care. It is well, therefore, if time permits, to lay the prescription aside for a minute or two, until it has cooled, as it were, and then examine it critically, as if it were the work of some one else.

It is always desirable for the physician to sign his name to the prescription, in order that, if there is any question about its propriety, the apothecary may know that a responsible party has written it, and that a compliance with its directions will not result to the compounder's detriment. Some physicians sign only their initials ; and this, doubtless, is generally sufficient in a small place, or in a large one if the doctor is a distinguished practitioner. But, even in these cases, it is far better to write the full name ; for prescriptions are often carried out of the town in which they are made, and beyond the boundaries of most men's fame ; and a failure to show a practical recognition of these facts, though perhaps really due to the proverbial modesty of medical men, may be construed by the evil-minded as an evidence of conceit. If the place be a sizable city, it is advisable to give the residence as well as the name, so that the druggist may, if he desires, readily consult the physician about the medicine intended. This is more frequently necessary than would be supposed by one unfamiliar with the subject. Occasionally it is helpful to know when a prescription was written; the date, therefore, should be inserted.

The exact quantity of the dose, the periods for its repetition, the method of taking, and all other necessary directions, should be written out at full length, and in the plainest possible language, for the apothecary to copy on the label. This is not only of great assistance to the patient and his attendants, who, with all their anxiety and the extraordinary cares which illness in the family always brings, are very liable to forget the small but important details of administration; but it is also an aid to the apothecary, in enabling him to detect errors in dose which he otherwise could not, and thus, perhaps, to save the physician from a mortifying predicament, and the patient from an aggravation of his sufferings. There are exceptional cases, however, in which it is better to rely on the memory of the patient than to label his medicine so distinctly as to arouse in the minds of others suspicions as to the character of his malady. In some cases, for example, we write "Wash" rather than "Injection," although the latter word is more closely descriptive of the character of the medicament, and the method of using it. The shorter word is sufficient for the purposes of the patient, and others are left in ignorance as to whether it is scalp, eyes, urethra, or some other part for which the lotion is designed.

Remedies to be employed topically should always be so marked, to distinguish them from those which are to be taken internally. Lack of attention to this point has sometimes resulted fatally to the patient. When a very powerful and concentrated medicine is ordered, it is a good idea to have it labelled "Poison," as a warning to careless persons. The direction, "To be used as ordered," though very common, is to be avoided ; it is entirely valueless, since it does not serve to recall to mind any thing except the fact that some directions have been given, which was well enough known before.

Some apothecaries have a space on their labels for the patient's name, and it would be well if the practice of writing the name on the prescription were more common. There would be less liability to mistakes in delivering packages to customers, reference to the apothecary's files would be somewhat facilitated, and, when there were two or more sick in the same household, the chance of the wrong medicine's being given to any one of them would be greatly diminished.

Unfortunately, on many accounts, it is the custom for apothecaries to refill prescriptions as often as they are requested to. Physicians sometimes complain of this practice, which, evidently, is frequently injurious to them and to their patients ; but, for the most part, they have only themselves to blame, because they have so long permitted the wrong without a protest. Apothecaries consider the transaction in a commercial light almost altogether, and generally have no idea of doing any one an injury. But, if the physician were to write across the face of his prescription "Not to be repeated," or "To be repeated only so many times," or some other words which would establish a limit to the legitimate renewals, it is hardly supposable that a pharmaceutist of respectability and honor, or even of moderate shrewdness, would disregard the reasonable request of one who alone is fully competent to judge of the therapeutic requirements of the case, and whose favor and esteem he can poorly afford to lose. It is not necessary to exercise this caution in all prescriptions ; in some cases the repetition may be left to the discretion of the patient. But, in ordering powerful drugs, thought should always be bestowed upon this point.

It is customary to employ certain domestic measures in administering the doses of medicines. Thus, a teaspoon is supposed to hold a fluidrachm ; a tablespoon, half a fluidounce. These implements are, however, by no means of constant size, varying often fifty or more per cent. from the regular standard. It is very desirable that patients should supply themselves with the graduated glasses which may now be easily obtained, and discard altogether the old and inaccurate measures.

In apportioning the quantities of the different elements of a prescription, the following rule will afford assistance : First write the names of the various ingredients, giving a line to each. Then, having decided upon the length of time that the patient will probably need to take the medicine, and determined the frequency of its administration, the whole number of doses is readily calculated. Multiply the dose of each constituent in turn by the whole number of doses, and write down each product in its proper line.

In directions to the apothecary, it is desirable to observe as much brevity as is consistent with perspicuity. He is supposed to understand pharmacy, and it is, therefore, unnecessary to give more than general directions about the various steps in the operation of compounding the medicine. The physician orders certain substances to be put together ; the precise method of doing this so as to obtain the best result it is the business of the pharmacist to know. The prescriber takes care that the articles are not incompatible and are capable of forming a proper mixture ; the rest may be left to the compounder.

The foregoing directions should be observed, whatever the language may be in which the prescription is indited. It is quite proper to write it in English, if one chooses. There are even some who inveigh acrimoniously against the practice of writing prescriptions in Latin, considering it an unnecessary trouble, a relic of a by-gone and less enlightened age, a pedantic display of useless knowledge, and, perhaps, other and still more objectionable things. But, nevertheless, it is a phenomenal occurrence to find a prescription written in English, that is, entirely in English, even by those who deprecate the use of Latin. They usually unconsciously allow something of the berated tongue to obtain entry into their prescriptions, and the result is a hodge-podge which would be amusing were it not so deplorable.

In spite of all objections, Latin is by far the best language for prescriptions. It is not subject to the variations which modern languages are continually undergoing, being, as it were, crystallized. It is consequently adopted as the language for scientific nomenclature, and formerly scientific works were written in it altogether. There would seem to be no reason why the names of drugs should be an exception to the otherwise universal rule, and Latin is therefore employed in naming the articles of the pharmacopœia. It is the only language in which it is practicable to write the international pharmacopœia, which is so important a desideratum. The advantage of a well-established language for scientific terminology is plainly seen in the greater definiteness with which medicines may be ordered in Latin. The Latin name for a drug is applied to no other, and one is sure to get what he desires if he has written for it under its scientific title, — provided, of course, that the pharmacist does his duty. But, in ordering certain articles by their English names, we are often uncertain with what we may be furnished, the terms used being frequently applied variously. Thus, if Indian Hemp be written, meaning *Apocynum Cannabinum,* a diuretic, diaphoretic, etc., there may be put up *Cannabis Indica,* a stimulant-narcotic. If we order Yellow Root, hoping to get *Xanthorrhiza,* a simple bitter, we may be disappointed by receiving *Hydrastis,* a diuretic. So the word Wintergreen is applied to *Chimaphila,* an astringent and tonic, and to *Gaultheria,* a carminative and stomachic. Checkerberry and Foxberry will bring us at one time the astringent and diuretic *Uva Ursi;* at another, the aromatic *Gaultheria.* Snakeroot is a name given to *Serpentaria, Cimicifuga, Senega, Asarum, Eryngium,* and other drugs ; and Stinkpoke is the somewhat descriptive appellation of agents of widely differing powers, such as *Dracontium, Chenopodium, Stramonium,* and *Polanisia Graveolens.* From these illustrations we see that the indefiniteness of an English name may occasion not merely inconvenience, but even disaster ; and, if there were no other reason for using Latin, this alone would be sufficient.

But these are not the only advantages which come from writing prescriptions in Latin. It is often desirable to keep the patient in ignorance of what he is taking. There is a prejudice in the minds of many people against the use of certain drugs, such as mercury, lead, etc. ; and the names of these often valuable remedies may be successfully concealed under their technical titles, without arousing a suspicion as to their true character. In most cases, indeed, it is better that the patient should not know the exact composition of his medicine. Although it may be the article which of all things is best adapted to his needs, it will be less likely to do him all the good of which it is capable, if he discovers that it is some common and, to his mind, ignoble weed, than if he, judging from its imposing name, conceives an idea of a rare and stately exotic. I would by no means be understood to advocate, in any case, the practice of deception with the sick, which, to say the best of it, is impolitic in the long run; nor would I defend the quackish habit which some physicians have of impressing their patients with a sense of their importance by grandiloquently airing their knowledge of technical expressions; but we ought not to ignore the advantages which arise from keeping our own counsel at times, and the benefit which may, in a purely incidental way, come from the feeling of wonder and awe which, in the mind of the average man, is associated with the unknown. As it would often be cruel to the patient to volunteer, or even allow to be extorted, a complete pathological description and prognosis of his case, so it is generally unwise to permit him to know just what he is taking for a remedy.

A very limited knowledge of Latin is sufficient to enable one to write prescriptions properly. The necessary vocabulary, though comprising over six hundred words, has been almost entirely learned already by the student who has studied his Materia Medica faithfully; and the chief difficulty to be encountered is in making the changes which are requisite to the correct grammatical wording of the directions to the apothecary. The careful study of the following simple rules will, it is believed, enable one previously unacquainted with Latin Grammar easily to write elegant prescriptions. The effort has been to reduce the subject to its lowest terms, to make it so readily comprehensible that lack of time to study Latin will be no excuse for a badly written prescription.

Very few verbs are used in prescriptions. These are mostly imperatives addressed to the apothecary. Some are very common, occurring in a majority of prescriptions; as *Recipe* (take), *Misce* (mix), *Signa* (mark or label), *Fiat* (let [it] be made), or *Fiant* (let [them] be made). Others are less common, but still often used, as *Adde* (add), *Bulliat* (let it boil), *Cola* (strain), *Divide* (divide), *Macera* (macerate), *Repetatur* (it may be repeated), *Solve* (dissolve), *Sufficit* (it suffices), and *Tere* (rub). These need undergo no changes.

The last remark applies also to prepositions, conjunctions, and adverbs, which are quite infrequent. The principal are *Cum* (with), *In* (in, or into), *Ad* (to, or up to), *Et* (and), and *Ana* (of each).

Almost all the words in prescriptions are nouns and adjectives.

There are five declensions, or methods of forming the cases, in Latin; but, as there are no pharmacopœial words of the fifth declension, we need consider but four. Each declension has six cases; but, as it is very rarely necessary to use more than three, the others will be ignored. It will be easier to commit the exceptions outright and arbitrarily, than to learn the rule for their formation.

The three cases which are most employed are the Nominative, which corresponds exactly to our English nominative; the Genitive, the counterpart of the English possessive, or objective with " of; " and the Accusative, which takes the place of the English objective after a verb or preposition. These cases are distinguished by their endings, the preceding portion of the word being called the stem. The stem may be found by dropping the ending of the genitive singular; and the several cases may, in most instances, be formed by adding to this stem the case-endings. In all the following examples the case-endings are printed in Italics.

FIRST DECLENSION.

All pharmacopœial nouns ending in **a** (excepting *Aspidosperma*, *Physostigma*, and *Theobroma*), are of the first declension, of the feminine gender, and are formed like *Rosa*.[1]

Singular Number.

Nominative	Rosa,	a rose.	**a**
Genitive	Rosæ,	of a rose.	**æ**
Accusative	Rosam,	a rose.	**am**

Plural Number.

Nominative	Rosæ,	roses.	**æ**
Genitive	Rosarum,	of roses.	**arum**
Accusative	Rosas,	roses.	**as**

It will be noticed that the stem Ros remains unchanged all through the declension. Particular pains

---

[1] There are two pharmacopœial nouns of the first declension which end in e; namely, *Aloë* and *Mastiche*. The case-endings in the singular are :

Nominative	**e,**
Genitive	**es,**
Accusative	**en.**

The plural is formed like that of *Rosa*.

should be taken to become perfectly familiar with the case-endings, for these are the great stumbling-blocks to students generally.

SECOND DECLENSION.

All pharmacopœial nouns ending in **us** (excepting *Rhus* and the three nouns of the fourth declension) are of the second declension, mostly of the masculine gender, and are formed like *Rubus.*

Singular Number.

Nominative	Rubus,	a blackberry.	**us**
Genitive	Rubi,	of a blackberry.	**i**
Accusative	Rubum,	a blackberry.	**um**

Plural Number.

Nominative	Rubi,	blackberries.	**i**
Genitive	Ruborum,	of blackberries.	**orum**
Accusative	Rubos,	blackberries.	**os**

All pharmacopœial nouns ending in **um** are of the second declension, of the neuter gender, and are formed like *Acidum.*[1]

---

[1] There are three pharmacopœial nouns of the second declension which end in **on**; namely, *Eriodictyon, Hæmatoxylon,* and *Toxicodendron.* The case-endings in the singular are:

Nominative	**on,**
Genitive	**i,**
Accusative	**on.**

The plural is declined like that of *Acidum.*

Singular Number.

Nominative	Acidum,	an acid.	**um**
Genitive	Acidi,	of an acid.	**i**
Accusative	Acidum,	an acid.	**um**

Plural Number.

Nominative	Acida,	acids.	**a**
Genitive	Acidorum,	of acids.	**orum**
Accusative	Acida,	acids.	**a**

Notice, here and everywhere, that the accusative of a neuter is always like the nominative of the same number.

———•———

THIRD DECLENSION.

Declinable pharmacopœial nouns having *other* nominative endings than **a, us,** and **um,** are (with five exceptions [1]) of the third declension. They are mostly masculines and feminines, and these are declined like *Liquor.*

Singular Number.

Nominative	Liquor,	a solution.	—
Genitive	Liquoris,	of a solution.	**is**
Accusative	Liquorem,	a solution.	**em**

Plural Number.

Nominative	Liquores,	solutions.	**es**
Genitive	Liquorum,	of solutions.	**um**
Accusative	Liquores,	solutions.	**es**

Some of them are neuter, and are declined like *Marmor.*

---

[1] The exceptions are the two nouns in **e,** of the first declension, and three in **on,** of the second, all of which have been previously considered.

Singular Number.

Nominative	Marmor,	marble.	—
Genitive	Marmoris, of	marble.	**is**
Accusative	Marmor,	marble.	—

Plural Number.

Nominative	Marmora,	marbles.	**a**
Genitive	Marmorum, of	marbles.	**um**
Accusative	Marmora,	marbles.	**a**

In the two examples given, the nominative is the stem, and there is no case-ending. In many other words a nominative ending, as **is** or **e**, occurs; in others still the nominative not only lacks an ending, but is less than, and sometimes otherwise different from, the stem. These can easily be learned by studying the list of words of the third declension in the Second Part of the book.

———◆———

FOURTH DECLENSION.

Three pharmacopœial nouns ending in **us** are of the fourth declension, and are formed like *Fructus.* Two of them, *Fructus* and *Spiritus,* are of the masculine gender, and one, *Quercus,* is feminine.

Singular Number.

Nominative	Fructus,	the fruit.	**us**
Genitive	Fructus,	of the fruit.	**us**
Accusative	Fructum,	the fruit.	**um**

Plural Number.

Nominative	Fructus,	the fruits.	**us**
Genitive	Fructuum, of	the fruits.	**uum**
Accusative	Fructus,	the fruits.	**us**

The following table will show at a glance the endings of these three cases in both numbers of all four declensions : —

Singular Number.

	FIRST DECLEN.	SECOND DECLEN.		THIRD DECLEN.		FOURTH DECLEN.
		Masc.	Neuter	Masc. & Fem	Neut.	
Nominative	a	us	um	(Various)		us
Genitive	æ	i		is		us
Accusative	am	um		em	Like Nom.	um

Plural Number.

	FIRST DECLEN.	SECOND DECLEN.		THIRD DECLEN.		FOURTH DECLEN.
Nominative	æ	i	a	es	a	us
Genitive	arum	orum		um		uum
Accusative	as	os	a	es	a	us

The plural cases are quite infrequently used in prescriptions, except in naming the quantities of the ingredients. The ablative case occurs in the pharmacopœia only after the preposition *cum*, and then only as follows : *cum Creta* (with Chalk), *cum Calce* (with Lime), *cum Ferro* (with Iron), *cum Hydrargyro* (with Mercury), *cum Magnesia* (with Magnesia). *Cum semisse* (with a half) is used often in prescriptions.

A few nouns employed in prescriptions are indeclinable, that is to say, have the same form in every case, both singular and plural. A list of them is given in the Second Part.

The adjectives used in prescriptions are declined like nouns, those ending in **a** like Rosa,[1] in **us** like Rubus,[2] in **um** like Acidum,[3] and all others like the nouns of the third declension.

---

[1] Excepting *una*, whose genitive is *unius*.

[2] Excepting *unus*, whose genitive is *unius*, and *fortius*, which is of the third declension.

[3] Excepting *unum*, whose genitive is *unius*.

Adjectives agree with the nouns to which they belong in gender, number, and case.

Sometimes adjectives are of the same declension as the nouns with which they agree, as in these illustrations: *Amygdala Amara*, both being of the first declension; *Acidum Tannicum*, both of the second declension; *Æther Fortior*, both of the third declension.

But very often adjectives are of different declensions from the nouns with which they agree. The following are examples of this statement: *Amygdaa Dulcis*, the noun of the first declension, the adjective of the third; *Veratrum Viride*, noun of the second, adjective of the third; *Calx Chlorata*, noun of the third, adjective of the first; *Sulphur Lotum*, noun of the third, adjective of the second.

Sometimes, as in English, a noun has more than one adjective agreeing with it, as *Extractum Sarsaparillæ Fluidum Compositum*.

To illustrate these directions, we will take an example of a prescription written in English, and render it in Latin.

Take of Sulphate of Iron one scruple,
    of Extract of Quassia two drachms.
Mix them and divide into twenty-five pills.
Mark. For Mr. John Jacens. Take one pill half an hour before each meal.
PETER PROBANG, M.D.,
21, III, 1875.   8 Laudanum Lane.

Translated into Latin, this would read as follows: —

Recipe Ferri Sulphatis scrupulum unum,
    Extracti Quassiæ drachmas duas.
Misce et in pilulas viginti quinque divide.
Signa. For Mr. John Jacens. Take one pill half an hour before each meal.
PETER PROBANG, M.D.,
21, III, 1875.   8 Laudanum Lane

Let us now examine this translation in detail, and see the reason for each step in the process.

It will be remembered that a prescription was defined to be a formula consisting of directions to an apothecary. We commence by commanding him to " take " definite quantities of certain things which we desire to have associated in the medicine. So we employ the imperative singular of the Latin verb *Recipio* (I take), which is *Recipe* (take thou). The subject (thou) it is as unnecessary to express in Latin as in English. Now, the first thing which he is to take is " one scruple " of a certain drug ; and, as " scruple," being the immediate object of " take," is in the objective case, the Latin equivalent must be in the corresponding case, namely, the accusative. *Scrupulus* is the Latin for scruple, and, as it is of the second declension, the accusative is *scrupulum*. So we have *Recipe scrupulum*. This would sufficiently indicate the number ; but it is customary to affix a numeral adjective to all the nouns denoting measure and weight, so we take the accusative of *unus* (one), which, likewise being of the second declension, is *unum*. It would not answer to take the accusative of *una*, which also means one ; for the adjective must agree with its noun in gender as well as in number and case, and *scrupulus* being masculine, needs an adjective of the same gender to go with it. The termination **us** shows *unus* to be masculine, while the final **a** of *una* stamps it as feminine. This makes *Recipe scrupulum unum*. The drug of which we want one scruple is the Sulphate of Iron, of which the pharmacopœial name is *Ferri Sulphas*. *Ferri* is the genitive of *Ferrum* (Iron), and means, therefore, " of Iron." *Sulphas* means Sulphate, or The Sulphate. The Latin order in many instances places the limiting genitive before the nominative, though the sense is the same whatever the arrangement may be. But as we write in English "one scruple *of* Sulphate of Iron," so we must change the word *Sulphas* (Sulphate) to mean "of Sulphate." This we can do by using the genitive case. Turning to the Second Part of the book, we find in the list of nouns of the third declension that the genitive of *Sulphas* is *Sulphatis*. So we now have *Recipe scrupulum unum Ferri Sulphatis*, or, to observe the usual order in prescriptions, by which the names of the ingredients are placed before the words designating the amount of each, *Recipe Ferri Sulphatis scrupulum unum*. The word *Ferri* needed no change, of course, already meaning exactly what we want, "of Iron."

In translating the second line of the prescription, we proceed in precisely the same way. Thus, as "drachms" is in the objective case after "take," we write the accusative plural of *drachma*, which is *drachmas*. As "two" drachms are ordered, we affix the accusative of *duæ*,[1] the feminine form of the Latin numeral which means two, thus making an agreement of gender between the adjective and noun, and have *drachmas duas*. The article of which this quantity is ordered is Extract of Quassia, in Latin *Extractum Quassiæ;* but as we write "*of* Extract of Quassia," we must use the genitive case of *Extractum*, which is *Extracti*. *Quassiæ*, the genitive of *Quassia*, means "of Quassia," and stands unchanged. The second line, then, will be *Drachmas duas Extracti Quassiæ*, or, to correspond with the arrangement of the first line, *Extracti Quassiæ drachmas duas*.

In rendering "Mix them" in Latin, we may omit the pronoun, as there could not be any consequent mistake, and write simply the second person singular

---

[1] See declension of numerals on page 49

imperative of *Misceo* (I mix), which is *Misce.* " And " is *et.* " Divide " is translated by the second person singular imperative of *Divido* (I divide), which is *Divide.* For " into " we substitute *in,* a preposition which is followed by the accusative case ; so we write after it *pilulas,* the accusative plural of *pilula* (a pill), and thus render the word " pills." The Latin for " twenty-five " is *viginti quinque,* an indeclinable numeral. Following the usage of the language which places the verb last, we have for this line, *Misce, et in pilulas viginti quinque divide.*

Next comes the direction " Mark," which we translate by *Signa,* the second person singular imperative of *Signo* (I mark). Now, every thing which follows this verb should be transferred to the label on the medicine. It is the directions to or about the patient, and these we want to have as plain to him as they can possibly be made. So we do not turn into Latin any thing which follows *Signa.* Let no one object that this is a mixing of tongues such as has been deprecated in a preceding page ; for the directions to the patient are, as far as the apothecary is concerned, to be regarded as so many arbitrary signs. Indeed, it is not impossible that they might well be hieroglyphics in certain cases. It undoubtedly sometimes happens that the directions to the patient are in a language which the apothecary does not understand ; and, in such a case, his duty is to copy the words between *Signa* and the doctor's signature *literatim.* In so doing he is simply following instructions, which are to mark on the label whatever follows *Signa.* It is the custom in some other countries for the physician to write the directions in Latin, and for the pharmaceutist to translate them into English on the label. Aside from the fact that this is not a strict observance of directions, the usage is undesirable, first, on the ground that the compounder may be unable to translate the Latin into the tongue which alone the patient and his attendants can understand; and, second, because the liability to mistake is somewhat increased by the passage of the orders through a second language. In the United States it is the nearly universal custom to write the directions for administration just as they are intended to be on the label. This practice is as different from the jumbling of languages which is often seen in the naming of the medicines in prescriptions, as are successive remarks of two people of different nationalities, each in his own vernacular, from the macaronic gabble of silly school-girls who like to air their little French and Italian on every occasion.

After this comes the address of the prescriber, and, finally, the date.

Now, here is a prescription written out in full, as hardly one in a million is written; for it is customary everywhere to adopt abbreviations for every part of the work. Some of these are desirable, others are permissible but generally to be avoided, and others still are never to be countenanced.

Those of the first class are desirable because they shorten the writing without diminishing its clearness Some of them are real abbreviations, others are arbitrary signs. *Recipe* is represented by its initial letter; but it is a common practice to draw a straight mark across the quirk of the R, making the character ℞. The origin of this habit is curious. The ancient physicians, who worshipped the now exiled gods of Olympus, were accustomed to commence their prescriptions with a prayer to Jove, whose blessing they invoked on the action of the medicine. Probably this petition was never very long, and we can easily believe that, following the tendency of prayers and oaths to diminish in length according to the frequency of their repetition, it rapidly lessened. At all events, we know that the expression of it finally dwindled to the brevity of the astronomical sign of Jupiter, ♃. When Christianity supplanted the older religion, the custom of soliciting divine approval of the dose continued, and prescriptions were headed with condensed acknowledgments of a supernatural being whose favor would make the medicine curative, and whose disapproval would render it of no avail. These supplications were compressed into AΩ, a prayer to the eternal beginning and end, the first and the last, the Alpha and Omega of all things; N. D., the initials of *Nomine Dei* (in the name of God); J. D., *Juvante Deo* (God helping); J. J., *Juvante Jesu* (Jesus helping); and, most admirable of all as regards conciseness, ✝, the simplest sign of the cross of Calvary. But, although Christianity has progressed, and the former theology is now remembered only as an interesting superstition of a childish age, the Christian symbols have fallen into complete desuetude, and the mark, which so many centuries ago represented a devout petition to the great thunderer, is still seen at the head of our prescriptions, modified by the addition of the perpendicular stroke, which makes it equally the initial of Recipe, and the prayer to Jove. *Octarius* (a pint) and *Congius* (a gallon) are reduced to their initials, O and C. *Quantum sufficit* (a sufficient quantity) is represented by *q. s. Minimum* (a minim) is indicated by *m*, or by ♏. *Granum* (a grain) is condensed into gr.; *gutta* (a drop), into gtt.; *semissis* (a half), and *cum semisse* (with a half), into ss; and *libra* (a pound), into ℔. Arbitrary signs have been adopted for the representation of *drachma* (a drachm), ℨ, *uncia* (an ounce), ℥, and *scrupulus* (a scruple), ℈; and, when a fluidrachm or a fluidounce is wanted, the letter f is placed before the sign for drachm or ounce, as the case may be. An abbreviation or sign stands for any case of the Latin noun which it represents. The Roman numerals are used instead of the full Latin numeral adjective; so we have i, v, x, c, d, etc. As I and J were interchangeable in the original Latin, it is customary to write j instead of i, when the latter would stand as the last letter in a numeral combination, thus, ij, vj, xij, instead of ii, vi, xii; but this is, of course, a matter of no considerable consequence. It will be observed that the lower-case characters are used instead of capitals.

Next, there are some abbreviations which are permissible. Most of the names designating the kinds of pharmaceutical preparations come under this head. Thus, we may make the first few letters of a noun or adjective stand for any of its cases, as *pil.* for *pilula, chart.* for *chartula, mist.* for *mistura, liq.* for *liquor, pulv.* for *pulvis, tinct.* for *tinctura, syr.* for *syrupus, aq.* for *aqua, comp.* for *compositus, composita,* or *compositum, fl.* for *fluidus, fluida,* or *fluidum, dil.* for *dilutus, diluta,* or *dilutum.* It is likewise very common to reduce the names of the drugs in the same way, as *Hydrarg.* for *Hydrargyrum, Morph.* for *Morphina, Bellad.* for *Belladonna, Ipecac.* for *Ipecacuanha, Antim.* for *Antimonium, Amyg.* for *Amygdala. Ana* is contracted into *aa.* A number of the verbs which are employed are abbreviated, *fiat* and *fiant* becoming *ft., divide* shortening into *div.,* and *misce* and *signa* dwindling into M. and S. respectively. A few of these are so obvious as almost to belong in the class of desirables.

Finally come those which are never to be tolerated, and they are put in this class of inexcusables be-

cause of their ambiguity. Examples are found in
Acid. Sulph., which may mean *Acidum Sulphuricum*
or *Acidum Sulphurosum; Hydr. Chlor.* which might be
Hydrargyri Chloridum, or *Hydras Chloralis; Acid.
Hydroc.*, which is equally an abbreviation of *Acidum
Hydrochloricum*, and *Acidum Hydrocyanicum*. One
who knows any thing of the physiological action of
these agents will see at once that here are chances
for mistakes which might be not only injurious, but
even deadly. The principle to guide us in all abbre-
viating is the rule of clearness. If a word when
abbreviated could possibly be mistaken for any
other, write it out in full. And, indeed, in all cases,
excepting those first mentioned, it is far better to
write every letter. There can then be no question
as to the meaning. If the objection is raised that
this method takes more time, it may be suggested
that when a physician's business is so extensive that
he cannot spare an extra minute on each prescription for the sake of protecting his patient from the
danger of taking the wrong medicine, it behooves
him to consider whether his duty to the sick and
to himself does not require such a reduction of
his work as will allow him to devote enough time
and attention to every case to treat it in all
respects with deliberate care. Human life and
health are too precious to be trifled with, and
hurry (I do not mean rapidity) in therapeutics is a
sin. Physicians who have long and, so far as they
know, safely abbreviated may scout these ideas, and
scoff at what they may think the pedantry of a fully
expressed prescription; but no such comments will
be made by apothecaries, who are so often perplexed
and harassed by these abridgments, which, if **the
truth** were to be told, owe their existence less **frequently** to lack of time than to ignorance.

Though it is a minor point, it is worth mentioning, that a prescription has a much more elegant appearance if written in accordance with the advice given above. As in other matters, such a consideration deserves attention. A bistoury may, perhaps, cut as well without as with a crocus polish; but the burnished surface is a satisfaction, and a surgeon likes to have his knife not only sharp, but shining.

The prescription which has been discussed might, then, be safely and correctly written as follows : —

R. Ferri Sulphatis ℈j,
Extracti Quassiæ ℥ij.
M. et in pil. xxv div.

S.   For Mr. John Jacens.   Take one pill half an hour before each meal.

PETER PROBANG, M.D.,

21, III, 1875.   8 Laudanum Lane.

But it would be more attractive in appearance if only the nouns and adjectives of weight and quantity were abbreviated.

Let us take another English prescription and translate it into Latin. The address and date may be omitted, as unnecessary to the example : —

Take of Fluid Extract of Ergot three and a half ounces,
    of Tincture of Digitalis half an ounce.
Mix.   Mark, Half a teaspoonful thrice daily.

"Take" becomes *Recipe.* "Fluid Extract of Ergot" is *Extractum Ergotæ Fluidum.* But we want the Latin equivalent of " *of* Fluid Extract of Ergot," which is found in the genitive form. *Extractum* and *Fluidum* both make their genitive by changing the terminal *um* into *i;* so "of Fluid Extract" is *Extracti Fluidi. Ergotæ* is the genitive of *Ergota,* and already means "of Ergot," so it undergoes no alteration. Preserving the original order, we have

Extracti Ergotæ Fluidi. "Ounces" being in the objective case after "Take," the Latin needs the accusative plural of *uncia* (an ounce) after *Recipe.* This is *uncias.* This word being feminine, we look for the feminine accusative of the Latin numeral for "three" (page 49), and get *tres.* "And a half" is equivalent to the Latin *cum semisse* (with a half). The first line, then, will stand, *Recipe Extracti Ergotæ Fluidi uncias tres cum semisse.*

"Tincture of Digitalis" is *Tinctura Digitalis.* In order to change this to "*of* Tincture of Digitalis," we put *Tinctura* into the genitive, which is done by making the ending *a* into *æ,* — *Tincturæ Digitalis. Digitalis,* already meaning what we desire, remains undisturbed. "Half an ounce" is *unciæ semissis, unciæ* being the genitive of *uncia,* and meaning "of an ounce," and *semissis* meaning "a half." But this needs to be changed into the accusative as the direct object of *Recipe. Semissis* has *semissem* for its accusative, and *unciæ,* being uninfluenced by the verb, continues the same. The second line will then read *Tincturæ Digitalis unciæ semissem.*

"Mix" and "Mark" become respectively *Misce* and *Signa,* as before, and the directions will be transcribed exactly as they stand. Employing the desirable abbreviations, we have the translation as follows : —

R. Extracti Ergotæ Fluidi ℥iijss,
　　Tincturæ Digitalis ℥ss.
Misce. Signa, Half a teaspoonful thrice daily.

Here is the formula for the Compound Cathartic Pills of the pharmacopœia (1880) : —

Take of Compound Extract of Colocynth thirty-two grains,
　　　　of Abstract of Jalap,
　　　　of Mild Chloride of Mercury, each, twenty-four
　　　　　　grains,

of Gamboge six grains,
of Water a sufficient quantity.
Mix.   Divide into twenty-four pills.

As in previous similar cases, the name of a drug of
which a preparation is used undergoes no change,
because it is already in the exact form which we
desire ; so " of Colocynth," " of Jalap," and " of
Mercury " remain as they are in the pharmacopœial
names of the several preparations ; namely, *Colocynthidis, Jalapæ,* and *Hydrargyri.* " Compound Extract," " Abstract," " Mild Chloride," " Gamboge,"
and " Water," being all in the objective after " of,"
must have their Latin .equivalents put into the genitive ; thus we have *Extractum Compositum* turned
into *Extracti Compositi, Abstractum* into *Abstracti,
Chloridum Mite* into *Chloridi Mitis, Cambogia* into
Cambogiæ, and *Aqua* into *Aquæ.* " Grains " in
every instance would be *grana,* the accusative plural
of *granum,* and the direct object of *Recipe ;* " each "
is *ana ;* " thirty-two " is *triginta dua (dua* being the
neuter numeral and agreeing with *grana*) ; " twenty-
four" is *viginti quatuor ;* " six " is *sex ;* and " a
sufficient quantity" is *quantum sufficit.* The rest
has been explained before.   The following is the
result : —

R. Extracti Colocynthidis Compositi gr. **xxxij**,
Abstracti Jalapæ,
Hydrargyri Chloridi Mitis, ana gr. **xxiv**,
Cambogiæ gr. **vj**,
Aquæ q. s.
Misce.   In pilulas **xxiv** divide.

Suppose we want to prescribe a dozen of these
pills, which, being officinal, are kept ready made in
all shops, and are known as *Pilulæ Catharticæ Com-
positæ.*   We write : —

R. Pilulas Catharticas Compositas **xij**.

Here it will be observed that the name of the medicine is written in the accusative case, instead of the genitive, as is usual ; for the reason that there is no noun of weight or capacity to stand as immediate object of *Recipe*, but only the name of the medicine itself, with a limiting numeral adjective agreeing with it. If we ordered pills by the pound or pint, we should then be obliged to put their name in the genitive ; as, for example, as follows : R. Pilularum Catharticarum Compositarum octarium unum ; that is, Take one pint of Compound Cathartic Pills.

Another example : —

> Take of Carbolic Acid two drachms,
> of Alcohol,
> of Glycerine, each, one ounce,
> of Water six ounces.
> Mix. Mark, Use as a lotion.

Employing the accredited abbreviations, and taking it for granted that the rules already repeatedly illustrated are understood, it will readily be seen how this becomes

> R. Acidi Carbolici ʒij,
>   Alcoholis,
>   Glycerini, ana ʒj,
>   Aquæ ʒvj.
> Misce. Signa, Use as a lotion.

Occasionally the physician, having decided upon the whole quantity of his prescription, finds that, after having written down the names and amounts of all the active elements, some inert substance is needed to make up the required bulk, or to act as vehicle for the rest. In such cases it is the custom of some, instead of reckoning the exact amount of the additional substance, to order the apothecary to put in enough of it to make the whole measure, or weigh, so much. This is usually expressed by the preposition *ad*, here meaning "up to." For example, take this prescription : —

> R. Potassii Bromidi ℥jss,
> 　Ammonii Bromidi ℥iv,
> 　Extracti Conii Fluidi ℥iv,
> 　Extracti Juglandis Fluidi ℥ij,
> 　Aquæ ad ℥vj.
> Misce.

Though this practice is quite common, and is proper enough in itself considered, it is not altogether un-objectionable. I have known at least one instance in which an apothecary, who was unfamiliar with this style of writing prescriptions, translated the Latin preposition by the verb which has the same pronunciation in English, and actually *added* a number of ounces of syrup where only a few drachms were ordered. Until we can confidently count on a more extensive knowledge than such compounders display, it will be safer to reckon the quantity of each ingredient ourselves.

A few words which are not pharmacopœial, and not names of medicines, are often convenient in prescriptions. The chief of those not already mentioned are *chartula* (a powder), *pars* (a part), *lagena* (a bottle), *scatula* (a box), *capsula* (a capsule), *æqualis* (equal). *Chartula* literally means "a little sheet of paper," but is used to designate one of the equal parts of a pulverized medicine enclosed in a bit of paper, and ordinarily called "a powder." *Pulvis* is the name applied to a powdered substance, *chartula* to a little package of it prepared as a dose. Thus, if we desire to give a patient several doses of Dover's Powder, we may write : —

> R. Pulveris Ipecacuanhæ et Opii ℨj.
> In chartulas sex divide.
> Signa, One at a dose.

Here we say, *In chartulas* instead of *In pulveres*, because we not only want the Dover's Powder divided into six parts, but we want each of these done up in a little paper. *Pars* is employed when we order a fraction of any measure or weight, as *grani partem sextum*, — the sixth part of a grain. *Lagena* is convenient in ordering some preparation which is usually kept in the shops in bottles of a given capacity, as the Solution of Citrate of Magnesium, which is put up in twelve-ounces bottles, one of which we may order thus : —

> R. Liquoris Magnesii Citratis lagenam.

Sometimes favorite preparations are kept on hand in little boxes, each containing a known number of lozenges, pills, or other dry solids ; and one of these packages may be had under the name of *scatula*. Medicines of disagreeable taste, which may be administered in small doses, are often advantageously enclosed in capsules of gelatine or jujube paste. When we desire this, we use the word *capsula*, just as in some other cases we do *chartula*. The numeral adjectives and adverbs will be found in the Second Part.

There are a few very common inaccuracies which seem worthy of mention. It is improper to write *Fiat Mistura* instead of *Misce*, unless the preparation is really to be a pharmacopœial *Mistura*, that is, a suspension of an insoluble substance in an aqueous fluid. It is incorrect to write *grs.* as the abbreviation for *grana*, because there is no *s* in the word which is shortened. The proper reduction is *gr.* for both singular and plural. So, also, *pilula* and *pilulæ* should be abridged into *pil.*, and not *pill.*   Once in a while a prescription is seen in which the *s* is left out of *Misce*, — an error which is suggestive of the superstitions and barbarisms of medicine hundreds of years ago.

It would be easy to multiply examples of prescription-writing, but it is believed that enough have been given to illustrate the principles which must be observed in the work.   The student is recommended to practise diligently in turning such English prescriptions as he may come across into proper Latin, and in correcting those which he finds are faulty.   As abbreviations and signs are universally allowed in certain parts of prescriptions, the main difficulty will be experienced in changing the pharmacopœial names from nominative into genitive.   Especial stress is, therefore, laid upon the necessity of learning the rules for the formation of this case, and fixing them in memory, as can be done only by persistent application and practice.

SECOND PART.

WORDS USED IN WRITING PRESCRIPTIONS.

In this part are collected the Latin words which are used in naming the drugs and preparations of the United States Pharmacopœia, and such unofficinal medicinal articles as are extensively ordered in prescriptions; also, other words which are necessary or convenient in prescription-writing. The botanical names of the plants from which vegetable medicines are derived are not given, unless they chance to be identical with the pharmacopœial names, for the reason that the latter only are used in prescriptions.

The following hints will assist in the use of this vocabulary : —

If a word ends in **a**, it probably will be found in List I. If not, it is most likely the nominative plural of some word in List III.

Words ending in **us** are mostly in List II. But some words in **us** are in List IV, and others in List V.

A final **um** generally points to List III. If not, it probably indicates a genitive plural.

If a word ends in **æ**, it is probably the genitive of some word in List I.

The termination **i** almost certainly indicates the genitive of a word in List II or List III.

The ending **is** usually means that the word is the genitive of some member of List IV.

LIST I.

FIRST DECLENSION.

Nouns and adjectives ending in **a**, declined like *Rosa* (see page 19).

All nouns and adjectives in **a** which are used in prescriptions are thus declined, excepting *Aspidosperma*, *Physostigma*, *Theobroma*, (see List IV), *una*, and *tria* (see page 49).

Acacia.
Alba.
Aloina.
Althæa.
Amara.
Americana.
Ammonia.
Ammoniata.
Amygdala.
Apomorphina.
Aqua.
Arnica.
Aromatica.
Asafœtida.
Atropina.
Avena.
Bacca.
Belladonna.
Berberina.
Bergamotta.
Betula.
Brayera.
Bryonia.
Burgundica.
Caffeina.
Calendula.
Calumba.

Cambogia.
Camphora.
Camphorata.
Capsula.
Cascara.
Cascarilla.
Cassia.
Castanea.
Cathartica.
Centifolia.
Cera.
Cetraria.
Charta.
Chartula.
Chimaphila.
Chirata.
Chlorata.
Cimicifuga,
Cinchona,
Cinchonina.
Cinchonidina.
Citrata.
Coca.
Cocaina.
Codeina.
Composita.
Convallaria.

Copaiba,
Creta.
Cubeba.
Deodorata.
Destillata.
Dimidia.
Drachma.
Dulcamara.
Elastica.
Ergota.
Fistula.
Flava.
Fluidrachma.
Fluiduncia.
Frangula.
Galla.
Gallica.
Gaultheria.
Gentiana.
Glabra.
Glycyrrhiza.
Grindelia.
Guarana.
Gutta.
Gutta-percha.
Hedeoma.
Herba.

Hydrastinina.
Hyoscina.
Hyoscyamina.
Ichthyocolla.
Ignatia.
Indica.
Inula.
Ipecacuanha.
Jalapa.
Kamala.
Krameria.
Lagena.
Lana.
Lappa.
Lavandula.
Leptandra.
Libra.
Liquida.
Lobelia.
Magnesia.
Magnolia.
Manna.
Massa.
Matricaria.
Medulla.
Melissa.
Mentha.
Mistura.
Monobromata.
Morphina.
Morrhua.
Myrcia.

Myristica.
Myrrha.
Narcotina.
Nigra.
Oleoresina.
Oliva.
Pareira.
Physostigmina.
Phytolacca.
Pilocarpina.
Pilula.
Pimenta.
Piperina.
Piperita.
Ponderosa.
Potassa.
Præparata.
Pulsatilla.
Purificata.
Purshiana.
Quassia.
Quillaja.
Quinina.
Quinidina.
Resina.
Rosa.
Rubra.
Ruta.
Sabina.
Salvia.
Sanguinaria.

Santonica.
Sarsaparilla.
Scatula.
Scilla.
Scutellaria.
Senega.
Senna.
Serpentaria.
Socotrina.
Soda.
Sparteina.
Spigelia.
Staphisagria.
Stillingia.
Strychnina.
Sulphurata.
Terebinthina.
Theobroma.
Thuja.
Tinctura.
Tolutana.
Tragacantha.
Uncia.
Uva.
Valeriana.
Vanilla.
Veratrina.
Viola.
Virginiana.
Vomica.
Zea.

Nouns ending in **e** (see foot-note, page 19).[1]

Aloe.   Mastiche.

---

[1] A number of neuter adjectives end in **e**, as *dulce, glaciale, mite*. (See List IV.)

LIST II.

SECOND DECLENSION.

Nouns and adjectives ending in **us**, declined like *Rubus* (see page 20).

All nouns and adjectives in **us** which are used in prescriptions are thus declined, excepting *Fortius* and *Rhus* (see List IV), the nouns of the fourth declension (see List V), and *unus* (see page 49).

[The (f.) after a word means that it is feminine.]

Aceticus.
Aromaticus.
Benzoinatus.
Calamus.
Caryophyllus.
Chondrus.
Coccus.
Compositus.
Congius.
Crocus.
Dilutus.
Dimidius.
Eucalyptus.
Euonymus.
Exsiccatus.
Ficus.
Flavus.
Fusus.

Granulatus.
Humulus.
Hydrosus.
Hyoscyamus.
Idæus.
Juniperus (f.).
Moschus.
Nitrosus.
Octarius.
Odoratus.
Opulus.
Phosphorus.
Pilocarpus.
Præcipitatus.
Prunus.
Purificatus.
Rhamnus.

Ricinus.
Rosmarinus.
Rubus.
Saccharatus.
Sambucus (f.).
Scoparius.
Scrupulus.
Strophanthus.
Succus.
Syrupus.
Tamarindus.
Thymus.
Tolutanus.
Trochiscus.
Ulmus (f.).
Ursus.
Vitellus.

LIST III.

SECOND DECLENSION.

Nouns and adjectives ending in **um**, declined like *Acidum* (see page 21).

All nouns and adjectives in **um** which are used in prescriptions are thus declined, excepting *unum* (see page 49).

Absinthium.
Absolutum.
Abstractum.
Acetanilidum.
Aceticum.
Acetum.
Acidum.
Aconitum.
Æthereum.
Album.
Alcoholicum.
Alkalinum.
Allium.
Aloinum.
Aluminum.
Amarum.
Ammoniacum.
Ammoniatum.
Ammonium.
Amylum.
Anisum.
Antimonium.
Apioleum.
Apocynum.
Aquosum.
Argentum.
Aromaticum.
Arsenosum.
Arsenum.

Aspidium.
Aurantium.
Aurum.
Balsamum.
Barium.
Benzinum.
Benzoicum.
Benzoinum.
Bismuthum.
Bisulphidum.
Boricum.
Boroglycerinum.
Bromidum.
Bromum.
Cadinum.
Calcium.
Cantharidatum.
Capsicum.
Carbolicum.
Carboneum.
Cardamomum.
Carum.
Caulophyllum.
Ceratum.
Cerium.
Cetaceum.
Chelidonium.
Chenopodium.
Chinoidinum.

Chloridum.
Chloroformum.
Chlorum.
Chromicum.
Chrysarobinum.
Cinnamomum.
Citricum.
Colchicum.
Collodium.
Compositum.
Conium.
Coriandum.
Corrosivum.
Creosotum.
Crudum.
Cuprum.
Cyanidum.
Cydonium.
Cypripedium.
Decoctum.
Denarcotisatum.
Deodoratum.
Despumatum.
Dialysatum.
Dilutum.
Dimidium.
Dioxidum.
Disulphidum.
Elaterinum.

Emplastrum.
Emulsum.
Eupatorium.
Expressum.
Exsiccatum.
Extractum.
Ferrocyanidum.
Ferrum.
Flavum.
Fluidum.
Fœniculum.
Folium.
Frumentum.
Galbanum.
Gallicum.
Gelsemium.
Geranium.
Glonoinum.
Glycerinum.
Glyceritum.
Glycyrrhizinum.
Gossypium.
Grammarium.
Granatum.
Granum.
Guaiacum.
Hydrargyrum.
Hydratum.
Hydriodicum.
Hydrobromicum.
Hydrochloricum.
Hydrocyanicum.
Hydrogenium.
Hypophosphoro-
    sum.
Illicium.
Infusum.
Ingluvinum.
Inspissatum.
Iodatum.
Iodidum.

Iodoformum.
Iodum.
Lacticum.
Lactucarium.
Lignum.
Linimentum.
Linum.
Liquidum.
Lithium.
Lotum.
Lupulinum.
Lycopodium.
Magnesium.
Maltum.
Manganum.
Marrubium.
Menispermum.
Mezereum.
Minimum.
Naphthalinum.
Nigrum.
Nitricum.
Nitroglycerinum.
Nitrohydrochlo-
    ricum.
Oleatum.
Oleicum.
Oleum.
Opium.
Origanum.
Ovum.
Oxidatum.
Oxidum.
Oxygenium.
Pancreatinum.
Paraldehydum.
Pepsinum.
Peruvianum.
Petrolatum.
Petroleum.
Phenacetinum.

Phosphidum.
Phosphoratum.
Phosphoricum.
Picrotoxinum.
Piperinum.
Plumbum.
Podophyllum.
Potassium.
Præcipitatum.
Prunifolium.
Prunum.
Purificatum.
Purum.
Pyrethrum.
Pyroxilinum.
Quantum.
Rectificatum.
Reductum.
Resorcinum.
Rheum.
Rubrum.
Saccharatum.
Saccharum.
Saigonicum.
Salicinum.
Salicylicum.
Santalum.
Santoninum.
Scammonium.
Sesamum.
Sevum.
Sodium.
Spissum.
Stearicum.
Stramonium.
Strontium.
Stypticum.
Sublimatum.
Succinum.
Sulphidum.
Sulphuratum.

Sulphuricum.	Tartaricum.	Veratrum.
Sulphurosum.	Terebenum.	Viturnum.
Suppositorium.	Terpinum.	Vinum.
Tabacum.	Tiglium.	Xanthoxylum.
Tanacetum.	Tolutanum.	Xericum.
Tannicum.	Triticum.	Zeylanicum.
Taraxacum.	Unguentum.	Zincum.

Nouns ending in **on** (see foot-note, page 20).

Eriodictyon.   Hæmatoxylon.
Erythroxylon.   Toxicodendron.

----◆----

LIST IV.

THIRD DECLENSION.

Nouns and adjectives of various endings, declined like *Liquor* (see page 21) or *Marmor* (see page 22).

The first column contains the nominative, the second the genitive, of each word. In the genitive column all but the case-ending **is** is the stem to which the proper ending of each case is affixed. The neuters are marked as such. (See rule about accusatives of neuters, page 21.)

These words are far more difficult to form than those of any other declension, and must, for the most part, be learned arbitrarily, by sheer force of memory. A little help may be found in the fact that more than one fourth of them end in **as**, and that of these all but one (*Asclepias*) change the **as** to **atis** in the genitive.

Acetas.   Acetatis.
Adeps.   Adipis.
Æqualis.   Æqualis.

Æther.	Ætheris.
Alcohol (neut.).	Alcoholis.[1]
Albumen (neut.).	Albuminis.
Alumen (neut.).	Aluminis.
Animalis.	Animalis.
Anthemis.	Anthemidis.
Antimonialis.	Antimonialis.
Arsenas.	Arsenatis.
Arsenis.	Arsenitis.
Asclepias.	Asclepiadis.
Aspidosperma (neut.).	Aspidospermatis.
Barbadensis.	Barbadensis.
Benzoas.	Benzoatis.
Bicarbonas.	Bicarbonatis.
Bichromas.	Bichromatis.
Bisulphas.	Bisulphatis.
Bisulphis.	Bisulphitis.
Bitartras.	Bitartratis.
Boras.	Boratis.
Bos.	Bovis.
Calx.	Calcis.
Canadensis.	Canadensis.
Cannabis.	Cánnabis.
Cantharis.	Cantharidis.
Carbo.	Carbonis.
Carbonas.	Carbonatis.
Chloral (neut.).	Chloralis.
Chloras.	Chloratis.
Citras.	Citratis.
Colocynthis.	Colocynthidis.
Confectio.	Confectionis.
Cortex.	Corticis.
Digitalis.	Digitalis.
Dulce (neut.).	Dulcis.
Dulcis.	Dulcis.
Effervescens.	Effervescentis.
Emulsio.	Emulsionis.
Erigeron.	Erigerontis.

---

[1] Considered indeclinable by some authorities.

Fel (neut.).	Fellis.
Flexile (neut.).	Flexilis.
Flos.	Floris.
Fortior.	Fortioris.
Fortius (neut.).	Fortioris.
Glaciale (neut.).	Glacialis.
Hamamelis.	Hamamelidis.
Hirudo.	Hirudinis.
Hydras.	Hydratis.
Hydrastis.	Hydrastis.
Hydrobromas.	Hydrobromatis.
Hydrochloras.	Hydrochloratis.
Hypophosphis.	Hypophosphitis.
Hyposulphis.	Hyposulphitis.
Iris.	Iridis.
Juglans.	Juglandis.
Lac (neut.).	Lactis.
Lactophosphas.	Lactophosphatis.
Lactas.	Lactatis.
Limon.	Limonis.
Liquor.	Liquoris.
Lotio.	Lotionis.
Macis.	Macidis.
Majalis.	Majalis.
Mel (neut.).	Mellis.
Mite (neut.).	Mitis.
Molle (neut.).	Mollis.
Mollis.	Mollis.
Mucilago.	Mucilaginis.
Nitras.	Nitratis.
Nitris.	Nitritis.
Nux.	Nucis.
Oxalas.	Oxalatis.
Pars.	Partis.
Pepo.	Peponis.
Permanganas.	Permanganatis.
Phosphas.	Phosphatis.
Physostigma (neut.).	Physostigmatis.
Piper (neut.).	Piperis.
Pix.	Picis.
Portense (neut.).	Portensis.

Pulvis. — Pulveris.
Pyrophosphas. — Pyrophosphatis.
Radix. — Radicis.
Recens. — Recentis.
Rhus. — Rhoïs *or* Roris.
Rumex. — Rumicis.
Salicylas. — Salicylatis.
Salix. — Salicis.
Santoninas. — Santoninatis.
Sapo. — Saponis.
Semen (neut.). — Seminis.
Semissis. — Semissis.
Silicas. — Silicatis.
Sinapis. — Sinapis.
Solubile (neut.). — Solubilis.
Solubilis. — Solubilis.
Styrax. — Styracis.
Subacetas. — Subacetatis.
Subcarbonas. — Subcarbonatis.
Subnitras. — Subnitratis.
Subsulphas. — Subsulphatis.
Sulphas. — Sulphatis.
Sulphis. — Sulphitis.
Sulphocarbolas. — Sulphocarbolatis.
Sulphur (neut.). — Sulphuris.
Tartras. — Tartratis.
Tersulphas. — Tersulphatis.
Theobroma (neut.). — Theobromatis.
Trituratio. — Triturationis.
Valerianas. — Valerianatis.
Vegetabilis. — Vegetabilis.
Venale (neut.). — Venalis.
Venalis. — Venalis.
Viride (neut.). — Viridis.
Viridis. — Viridis.
Volatile (neut.). — Volatilis.
Zingiber (neut.). — Zingiberis.

LIST V.

FOURTH DECLENSION.

Nouns ending in **us**, which are declined like *Fructus* (see page 22). They are exceptions to the rule that words ending in **us** are declined like *Rubus*.

Cornus. Fructus. Quercus. Spiritus.

———♦———

LIST VI.

INDECLINABLE NOUNS.

In addition to those words which are universally treated as indeclinable, there are included in this list some words of recent origin, which are not pharmacopœial and, consequently, have not yet been officially located by the only authority recognized as final in such matters in America; but analogy seems to justify placing them in this group.

Amyl.
Azedarach.
Buchu.
Cajuputi.
Catechu.
Cusso.
Diachylon.
Elixir.
Eucalyptol.
Hydronaphthol.
Kino.

Matico.
Menthol.
Methyl.
Naphthol.
Phenol.
Pyrogallol.
Quebracho.
Salol.
Sassafras.
Sumbul.
Thymol.

LIST VII,

NUMERAL ADJECTIVES.

CARDINALS.

All indeclinable, excepting *unus, duo, tres, mille,* and those denoting hundreds.

Unus,	one.	Viginti,	twenty.
Duo,	two.	Triginta,	thirty.
Tres,	three.	Quadraginta,	forty.
Quatuor,	four.	Quinquaginta,	fifty.
Quinque,	five.	Sexaginta,	sixty.
Sex,	six.	Septuaginta,	seventy.
Septem,	seven.	Octoginta,	eighty.
Octo,	eight.	Nonaginta,	ninety.
Novem,	nine.	Centum,	a hundred.
Decem,	ten.	Ducenti,	two hundred.
Undecim,	eleven.	Trecenti,	three hundred.
Duodecim,	twelve.	Quadringenti,	four hundred.
Tredecim,	thirteen.	Quingenti,	five hundred.
Quatuordecim,	fourteen.	Sexcenti,	six hundred.
Quindecim,	fifteen.	Septingenti,	seven hundred.
Sexdecim,	sixteen.	Octingenti,	eight hundred.
Septendecim,	seventeen.	Nongenti,	nine hundred.
Octodecim,	eighteen.	Mille,	a thousand.
Novendecim,	nineteen.		

To form the numbers between twenty and thirty, between thirty and forty, and so on, the English method is followed, the larger number being placed first. Thus, "twenty-one" becomes *viginti unus;* "fifty-six," *quinquaginta sex;* "seventy-four," *septuaginta quatuor.*

To express a given number of thousands we proceed as in English, placing the smaller numeral first. Thus, "ten thousand" becomes *decem millia.*

Combinations of numerals are made by the use of the conjunction *et*, "and."

The words for "one," "two," and "three" must agree with their nouns in gender, as well as in case, and the same holds good for those indicating hundreds.

Unus is thus declined : —

	Masculine.	Feminine.	Neuter.
Nominative	unus	una	unum
Genitive	unins	unius	unius
Accusative	unum	unam	unum

Duo is thus declined : —

	Masculine.	Feminine.	Neuter.
Nominative	duo	duæ	duo
Genitive	duorum	duarum	duorum
Accusative	duos	duas	duo

Tres is thus declined : —

	Masculine.	Feminine.	Neuter.
Nominative	tres	tres	tria
Genitive	trium	trium	trium
Accusative	tres	tres	tria

The cardinals denoting hundreds are declined in the masculine form (which alone is given in the list) like the plural of *Rubus*, in the feminine like that of *Rosa*, and in the neuter like that of *Acidum*.

For illustration, we will take *trecenti*, "three hundred" : —

	Masculine.	Feminine.	Neuter.
Nominative	trecenti	trecentæ	trecenta
Genitive	trecentorum	trecentarum	trecentorum
Accusative	trecentos	trecentas	trecenta

Mille, a thousand, is a neuter of the third declension, its genitive singular being *millis*, "of a thousand," and its genitive plural, *millium*, "of thousands."

Ordinals.

Only the masculine form of each is given; but each has a feminine, ending in **a** instead of **us**, and a neuter, ending in **um** instead of **us**. The masculines are declined like *Rubus* (see page 20), the feminines like *Rosa* (see page 19), and the neuters like *Acidum* (see page 21).

Primus	first.
Secundus	second.
Tertius	third.
Quartus	fourth.
Quintus	fifth.
Sextus	sixth.
Septimus	seventh.
Octavus	eighth.
Nonus	ninth.
Decimus	tenth.
Undecimus	eleventh.
Duodecimus	twelfth.
Tertius decimus	thirteenth.
Quartus decimus	fourteenth.
Quintus decimus	fifteenth.
Sextus decimus	sixteenth.
Septimus decimus	seventeenth.
Octavus decimus	eighteenth.
Nonus decimus	nineteenth.
Vicesimus	twentieth.
Vicesimus primus	twenty-first.
Vicesimus secundus	twenty-second.
Tricesimus	thirtieth.
Quadragesimus	fortieth.
Quinquagesimus	fiftieth.
Sexagesimus	sixtieth.
Septuagesimus	seventieth.
Octogesimus	eightieth.
Nonagesimus	ninetieth.
Centesimus	one hundredth.

LIST VIII.

VERBS.

Adde	add.
Bulliat	let (it) boil.
Cola	strain.
Divide	divide.
Fiat	let (it) be made.
Fiant	let (them) be made.
Macera	macerate.
Misce	mix.
Recipe	take.
Repetatur	let (it) be repeated.
Signa	mark, *or* label.
Solve	dissolve.
Sufficit	(it) suffices.
Tere	rub.

LIST IX.

CONJUNCTIONS, PREPOSITIONS, AND ADVERBS.

Ad	to
Ana	of each.
Cum	with.
Et	and.
In	into, *or* up to.
Non	not.
Vel	or.

Numeral Adverbs.

Semel	once.
Bis	twice.
Ter	thrice.
Quater	four times.
Quinquies	five times.
Sexies	six times.
Septies	seven times.
Octies	eight times.
Novies	nine times.
Decies	ten times.

APPENDIX.

THE METRIC SYSTEM IN PRESCRIPTIONS.

SINCE the body of this book was written, so much attention has been bestowed upon the metric system as to make it desirable to add a few words on its use in prescription writing. It is not intended to discuss the merits or disadvantages of this method of reckoning; it is sufficient to know that an acquaintance with it is rapidly becoming an absolute necessity to every man who wants to read medical works intelligently.

In the transition stage from the old system of weights and measures to the new, we must know both; but the difficulty of translating one into the terms of the other is very slight. In prescription writing it is by far the best plan to do away with the measures of volume, and use only the measures of weight. This does not make it necessary to remember the specific gravity of each separate liquid preparation; for in most cases sufficient accuracy is attained by reckoning all as if they were water, except the syrups, which are about one-third heavier, chloroform, which is one-half heavier, and ether, which is one-third lighter. Of the weights we need employ only the gram, which is the unit, the centigram, the one-hundredth part of a gram, and the milligram, the one-thousandth part of a gram; which correspond exactly with the commonest terms in our United States money, namely, the dollar, the unit, cent (or centidollar, to make the nomenclature structurally correspondent in all respects), the one-hundredth part of a dollar, and mill (millidollar), the one-thousandth part of a dollar. A gram being a little more than fifteen grains, a grain or minim is about .065 of a gram, or sixty-five milligrams; a drachm or fluidrachm is a trifle less than four (4) grams; and an ounce or fluid ounce a little less than thirty-two (32) grams. If we drop the .005, the most inconvenient part of the fraction, and call .06 of a gram (six centigrams) a grain, we shall be sufficiently near for the practical purposes of ordinary medication, making our small error on the safe side, by giving the patient less than he would be likely to get by the present method. We generally deviate, too, in the right direction in calling four grams a drachm, and thirty-two grams an ounce; for the substances given in drachms and ounces are usually the vehicle, or, if not that, are of such a nature that so small an increase of the dose would make no difference in the effect. In administering medicines there is, in the most favorable circumstances, a certain general sphere of error which is inevitable. We cannot precisely apportion doses to the needs of the sick; and variations like those which will result from the ready method of translation given above are no greater than occur many times a day in the practice of a busy physician who does not diminish or increase the conventional grain dose of a drug according as the patient is a few pounds lighter or heavier than the average, has a pulse a few beats less or more, or a nervous susceptibility a trifle below or above the common.

The use of the Arabic characters in metrically written prescriptions is essential to ready clearness and to comfort, as the fractions of a gram could be represented by the Roman numerals only by a tedious and, to many, not very intelligible combination. It cannot with much force be asserted that the use of these figures is a mixing of tongues such as has been objected to in the preceding pages; for these characters are hardly more arbitrary as signs for words than are the Roman. For instance, quadraginta would not seem to be more naturally represented by XL than by 40. It is best to separate the whole numbers from the fractions by the decimal line, as we do in writing a column of dollars and cents. Gram. (the abbreviation for Grammarium and Grammaria, the Latin for gram and grams respectively) should be written with a capital initial and after the number indicating the quantity, so as to reduce to a minimum the chance of the apothecary's confounding it with gr. (the abbreviation for granum and grana) which is placed before the number.

Example : —

R. Strychninæ Sulphatis	0|05	Gram.
Quininæ Bisulphatis	2|00	"
Acidi Phosphorici Diluti	20|00	"
Syrupi Pruni Virginianæ	70|00	"
Aquæ Destillatæ	50|00	"

Misce.

www.ingramcontent.com/pod-product-compliance
Lightning Source LLC
Chambersburg PA
CBHW022035080426
42733CB00007B/840